A MASTERPIECE

THE MUSEUM CARTOON COLLECTION

"Now can we have an eating experience?"

AMERICAN ASSOCIATION OF MUSEUMS | AAM100

Featuring Cartoons from

THE NEW YORKER

PUBLISHED BY THE CARTOON BANK

To purchase Custom Cartoon Books, framed prints of cartoons and covers, or to license
cartoons for use in periodicals, Web sites, or other media, please contact The Cartoon Bank,
a *New Yorker Magazine* Company, Tel: 800-897-8666, or (914) 478-5527, Fax: (914) 478-5604,
E-mail: custombooks@cartoonbank.com, Web: www.cartoonbank.com.

First edition published 2006

A MASTERPIECE

THE MUSEUM CARTOON COLLECTION

AMERICAN ASSOCIATION OF MUSEUMS | AAM**100**

Featuring Cartoons from
THE NEW YORKER

AAM100

What's So Funny about Museums Anyway?

Museums are serious institutions devoted to public service, education and the stewardship of our shared cultural heritage. They are havens of creativity, intelligence, history and science. So where is the humor in that?

Right here. This special anniversary collection, published on the occasion of AAM's centennial, features cartoons from *The New Yorker* spanning more than 70 years, from 1930 to 2005. The selections enclosed depict the silent humors of the museum experience, the funny ways in which we use museums as a space to interact and react.

AAM is pleased to publish this volume in thanks to all of our friends, colleagues and supporters: the thousands of dedicated professionals who work in museums of every type and size all across the globe, the funders and policy makers, and of course the millions of visitors who grace our museums every year.

This humorous collection allows all of us in the museum field a moment of laughter in between the moments of forging ahead to provide the community with a place that encourages education and inspiration. Laughter is, after all, one of the best ways of getting us to pause and examine the subtleties of our everyday experiences. It is a wonderful reminder of our shared humanity. We hope that these cartoons will help all of us do that. Enjoy!

Edward H. Able, Jr.
President and CEO

"Hey, how do you get out of this thing?"

"*We've already done this room. I remember that fire extinguisher.*"

"It must be <u>pouring</u> outside."

"Personally, I'm a doer."

"Frieze!"

"On rainy days, I always get this pain right through here."

"I used to like _everything_ before I took my art-appreciation course."

"Tell us again about Monet, Grandpa."

FEEDING TIME
3:30

"Absolutely not. I don't give my provenance over the phone."

"*This place isn't bad during the week, but on weekends it turns into a zoo.*"

"Well, it was sort of like a cook-out."

"Here's one you'll understand."

"I love the convenience, but the roaming charges are killing me."

"That? That's where I had to cut my way out."

"*I know more about art than you do, so I'll tell you what to like.*"

"You've let more than your Met membership slip, haven't you, Lorna?"

"Where ever did you get that lovely band?"

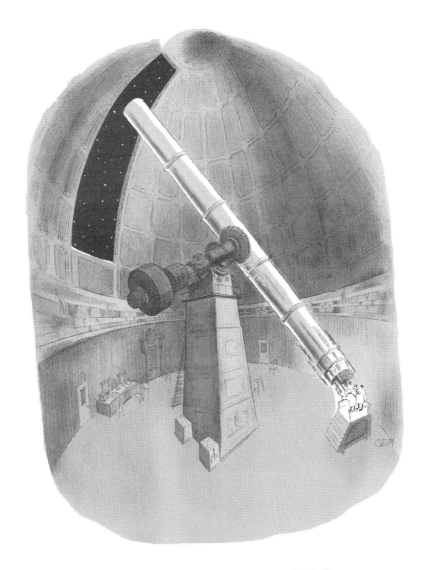

"What I like is the way they twinkle."

"Why can't someone design a museum that doesn't have to be explained?"

*"If you are under eighteen years of age and unaccompanied
by an adult, please move on to the next painting."*

"We haven't, of course, but I have the strangest feeling that we've been here before."

"Believe me, you're just thinking about it too much."

"Edgar, don't you think it's time you donated a wing somewhere?"

CHRISTO PAYS A VISIT TO CHESTER AND ELLIE SHUMWAY

"Well, they certainly have brightened things up around here!"

"*Miss Crutchfield, have you gone mad?*"

"Go deep!"

"Whew! I dreamed we'd been released into the wild!"

"Look, I'd rather be free, too, but at least we're not in a zoo anymore."

"'Born in conservation,' if you don't mind.
'Captivity' has negative connotations."

"Now can we have an eating experience?"

"Roger has always been text-driven."

"It's nice, but I never smile like that. I smile like this."

"I have a couple of other projects I'm excited about."

"*You're kidding. I thought it was Friday.*"

"Makes you feel you're not so old after all."

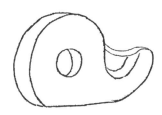

S. GROSS

"I don't care if she is a tape dispenser. I love her."

"Why, no. I've never thought of putting funny little captions on the bottom."

"You've got mail."

"Memo to self: 'Feathers?'"

"*I wish you'd stop trying to gross everybody out.*"

"*I think he was a celebrity.*"

"We're not certain why they disappeared, but archeologists speculate that it may have had something to do with their size."

"I'm beginning to suspect that someone ghosted <u>his</u> thesis."

"*Whenever you're ready.*"

"I hereby sentence you to the Vermeer show on a Saturday afternoon."

"Instead of 'It sucks' you could say, 'It doesn't speak to me.'"

"What I do as an artist is take an ordinary object—say, a lamppost—and, by urinating on it, transform it into something that is uniquely my own."

"He didn't do anything, Gregory. This is a zoo."

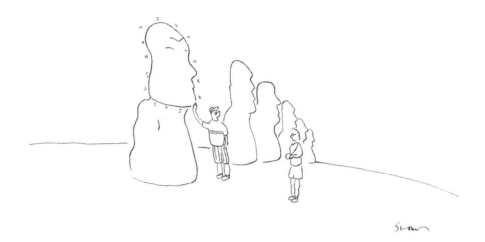

"They're bobbleheads."

"I can't imagine bringing a child into the current art world."

"They got extinct because they didn't listen to their mommies."

"I don't know if he's a great artist, but he's certainly annoying."

"See? While <u>your</u> unsurpassed collection of <u>gum wrappers</u> sits idle!"

"*Remember—anything said on this butte stays on this butte!*"

"That's right, honey—it was a wardrobe malfunction."

"Any impressionists in this crowd?"

THE LAST TEMPTATION OF CHRISTO

WEYANT

"He makes it look easy."

"She's not naked, Jake, she's French."

"Where does he get all his ideas?"

THE HUDSON RIVER SCHOOL
TAKES A WORKING VACATION.

"How do you know when you're done appreciating?"

"*Someday this cave could be worth plenty.*"

"Mommy says she's lived in a cage without bars for years."

"You're on next. Break a leg!"

"He's big, but he's no Chuck Close."

"More lithium."

"It's museum-store quality."

"I tried art for a while back in the eighties, but, talk about a jungle..."

"We had to let the animals go. No one informed them of their rights when they were arrested."

"Could we be getting a little too museum-quality?"

"I guess cats just can't appreciate Frank Gehry."

"I didn't go to the office today. I went to the zoo."

INDEX OF ARTISTS

Front cover: Mike Twohy
Front jacket flap: Robert Mankoff
Back cover: Joseph Mirachi
Back jacket flap: Mike Twohy